Guide to Pro Se
Civil Litigation

Angela Gomez

2025

Disclaimer: This book is for informational purposes only. Nothing contained herein should be construed as an attempt to provide legal advice. This book is not in any way a substitute for legal advice from a licensed attorney

Table of Contents

I. Introduction

The decision to represent oneself (pro se litigation) is a personal one, but this task can be especially daunting and is often not nearly as easy as some might think. The reasons one might choose to represent themselves often revolve around the significant costs of hiring an attorney, but litigation itself can be very costly. Aside from the cost, it has been said that very few litigants that have gone pro se, have actually prevailed. It is for this reason that I have chosen to write this book. I believe that this is a feat which can be taken on and that many people might succeed if given the proper information prior to finding themselves knee deep in procedures they know nothing about. With proper training,i. pro se litigants might find themselves succeeding and overcoming obstacles that they never believed possible. That being said, if you decide to take on your own case pro se, be prepared to study the rules of procedure, whether that be at the federal, state, or local level depending on your case. Before you head into filing a complaint, you should know these rules like the back of your hand, and, if you are wise, you will have already made significant preparations for the proceedings that will come before you.

It is my goal to arm you with the information that is necessary to take on your own case, and to handle it like a pro. The information contained within will only pertain to civil matters (versus criminal), and much of it pertains to federal suits. However, many state rules of procedures share the uniform structure of the federal rules, so this information can be useful in preparation for any case. You will also need to learn how to locate the local rules of procedure where you will be proceeding with your case. This book does not suffice for legal advice and one would be well advised to consult with a licensed attorney even if you are planning to go pro se. In addition to federal, state, and local rules of procedure, you will need to know about the prevailing law as it pertains to your case, or specific set of facts. You will also need to understand the basics of civil law, and what kind of case is worth pursuing.

II. Initial Considerations

Prior to deciding whether to file a claim against an individual or a business or corporation, you should consider the alternatives to filing a lawsuit, such as mediation and alternative dispute resolution. You may also consider whether taking your complaint to a government agency such as the Equal Employment Opportunity Commission or the Consumer Protection Agency would be a more appropriate action.

You should consider whether you really have a valid claim against the person you want to sue. To be able to recover in a civil suit, you will be required to show that someone broke the law, and that you were personally harmed as a result of that violation of law. You will also need to consider whether the statute of limitations has lapsed which would be a permanent bar to recovery. The general statute of limitations for federal civil suits under 28 U.S. Code § 1658 is four years for most cases, but this can be different based on what type of case you have. It is always best to consult with an attorney. The statute of limitations generally begins to run the moment you learn of the injury, and not necessarily the date that the injury occurred. The statute of limitations for most personal injury cases in Kentucky is only one year, so you will need to research the law in your area to be certain.

You will also need to be aware of what is legally required to become a pro se litigant. First and foremost, you must demonstrate to the judge that you have the mental capacity to take on such a feat and that you understand the legal consequences should you not prevail. You will need to show a strict adherence to the rules of the court and to be aware of all filing procedures and deadlines. You must show proper conduct and know that missing a deadline could cause you to lose your case. You should understand that there is a sharp learning curve and that pro se litigation involves an enormous time commitment. There will likely be costs associated with litigation that you cannot recover even if you win your case. These costs may include the hiring of expert witnesses or securing other information through the discovery process.

Pro Se Tips:

1. Read everything carefully and keep impeccable records
2. Keep a physical calendar and mark all deadlines and filing dates
3. Keep both paper and electronic copies of documents in case of loss of access to either
4. Check drafts of your papers with a friend to ensure clarity
5. Double check that the court has your correct contact information
6. Remember to keep personally identifying information, ie. dates of birth out of your papers

III. Before You File - Jurisdiction

You must be certain before you file your complaint that it is being filed in the correct court. Subject matter jurisdiction is determined by the subject of your lawsuit. If there is a federal question, such as a Civil Rights issue, then the federal courts have automatic jurisdiction. If the amount in controversy exceeds $75,000, and all of the plaintiffs are located in different states, then the federal court also has subject matter jurisdiction. If the case does not meet these requirements, then the case should be brought in state court. The subject matter and amount in controversy usually determine where to file your complaint in state court whether that be at the circuit or district court. At the federal level, all district courts are trial courts.

In addition to subject matter jurisdiction, you need to know which court has power over the person you are trying to sue. This is called personal jurisdiction. This is usually where the defendant lives or where they personally did something in that state which is the reason for the lawsuit. It may also be established if their activities have significant effects on a particular state. These factors allow a court to have personal jurisdiction over someone. You will need to file your lawsuit in the federal district where this personal jurisdiction lies. You may not sue a government employee acting in a government capacity, as they are immune, and you may not sue a government agency. Venue refers to the geographical location where the lawsuit is filed.

IV. Procedural Rules

Rules of Civil Procedure are sets of rules that you should become very familiar with should you choose to represent yourself in a court of law. The Federal Rules of Civil Procedure govern all federal courts and the Federal Rules of Evidence govern all discovery procedures in a federal lawsuit. You would be wise to purchase a copy of both as you follow along with this text. There you will find what types of evidence is considered admissible so you will not waste time on evidence that is not. You would be advised by any court to study and adhere to these rules when you decide to go pro se. In a state level civil suit, you will also find local Civil Rules, and each district court has its own set. In addition, most U.S. Federal Judges publish their own standing rules and you should obtain a copy of when you file your complaint. It is your job to locate and study all the procedural rules and standing orders as you will not be excused in court for not knowing. It is up to you to advocate for yourself through knowledge and due diligence.

V. Substantive Law

Through the study of substantive law, you will learn what you need to prove each element of your claim. Sources of substantive law include case law (common law), constitutions, statutes, and administrative regulations. Any of these may apply to your case, but the elements needed to prove your claim (such as what constitutes a breach of contract) are likely going to be found in case law. Be sure to note whether the case is current and to check for treatment in courts with a relationship to yours. Access to current case law can be obtained through public law libraries (often at your local university) in your area. You may also gain electronic access through websites such as Westlaw or LexisNexis.

VI. Drafting the Complaint

The complaint tells the court (and the defendant) how and why you believe the defendant violated the law and how this was the cause of your injury. The first step to drafting any complaint is to consult with the procedural rules in the court where you will be filing your complaint. The Federal and State Rules of Civil Procedure (of course) govern the required components of a complaint, but there may be additional rules that apply to your case, such as numbering each line in the left side margin. Be sure that you know every single rule or risk having your case thrown out. Whenever possible, look for forms and pleadings that you may refer to when drafting your documents. A civil complaint form for federal district court can be found here: https://www.uscourts.gov/forms-rules/forms/civil-pro-se-forms

Almost always, the first page should include the name, address, telephone and fax numbers, as well as the email addresses for each plaintiff. It should also include a case caption. The document should be titled "COMPLAINT", and should list the names of each defendant. You should include "Case No. __________" using an underscore to allow for a written entry of a new case number even though one does not yet exist. The placement of these all will depend on the specific court in which you are filing your suit, so be sure to find a sample. If you are asking for a jury trial, your complaint should include that information on the first page.

In numbered paragraphs, your complaint should include:

1. An explanation of how the court has jurisdiction over your case.
2. An explanation as to why you have chosen the correct venue.
3. A statement of any relevance to district or circuit
4. Identify the parties
5. A statement of the important facts
6. A statement of the laws that you think the defendant broke
7. If you have multiple claims, you should state each claim separately ie. “Claim 1” and “Claim 2”
8. Request for Relief - Explain what you want the court to do including damages
9. Demand for a jury trial, if you want, if not be sure to watch for the deadline to request one
10. Your signature

Your signature on a complaint certifies that the claim is being made in good faith and that you believe you have a valid claim. You are stating that you do not intend to harass the defendant, and that you have good reason to believe all the information is true. Some states and federal courts may make you pay court costs and fines for frivolous arguments which lack factual investigation. This information can be found in Rule 11 of the Federal Rules of Civil Procedure.

VII. Filing Your Complaint

Before you file, be sure to have the required number of copies with you if you physically go to the clerk's office. For the Northern District of California, you will need one copy marked "Chambers" for the judge, and two additional copies. Be sure to have the correct change. If you wish to e-file your complaint, in this district you will need prior permission from the court to use the e-filing system. You should also check for important rules for drop boxes. If you wish, you may fill out an application to proceed in Forma Pauperis. If your request is granted, you may not have to pay the filing fee. Be prepared to provide the court with information on your current employment, income, and general financial situation. An application to proceed In Forma Pauperis can be found here: https://cand.uscourts.gov/forms/civil-forms/ Upon filing your complaint, it is important to ask (at this time) if there are any judges standing orders that you need to be aware of, and if there is anything you need to do to proceed pro se in that particular court.

The federal court uses a Public Access to Court Electronic Records (PACER) system where you may review the docket. The docket should contain the names and addresses of all attorneys and unrepresented persons in a lawsuit. As well, it should contain a record of all documents, stored by title, in chronological order by the date the document was filed. Be sure to check the docket regularly after filing your complaint to be sure you have received copies of all filings, and that all documents that you have filed have been entered. PACER is available at computer centers found in the federal courthouse and is also accessible from any computer with an internet connection once you have made an account.

VIII. Serving Your Complaint

Pro Se litigants who have been given permission to proceed in forma pauperis will have their complaints served by the U.S. Marshall's Service. Otherwise, you must follow the process as outlined in the rules of procedure. Please take note that the rules for serving a complaint are different from the rules for serving other documents. A complaint may be served by any person who is at least 18 years old that is not a party to the lawsuit. A complaint not properly served can result in a dismissal or default judgement, so be very careful here. First, you need to obtain a summons from the court. You can download the Summons in a Civil Action for federal court from here: https://cand.uscourts.gov/forms/civil-forms/ The court must sign, seal, and issue the summons to the plaintiff before it can be served on the defendant. You may also find a civil cover sheet for download from the court's website. One summons may list all defendants, or each summons may be prepared separately. If you are proceeding in state court, check your local rules for specifics. The county clerk is usually happy to assist with these types of issues. All defendants must be served within 90 days of the issuance of the summons.

Steps to Serving a Complaint:

1. Request a Summons in a Civil Action form from the clerk or download one from the court's website

2. Present the summons to the court to be signed, sealed, and issued
3. Gather all required documents.

   You will need:

   A, The complaint

   B. The summons issued by the court

   C. Order setting case management - given to you by the clerk

   D. Judges Standing Orders

   E. If you are assigned a magistrate judge - Forms for consent to proceedings handled by a magistrate judge
4. Serve all defendants within 90 days.
5. File a certificate (or proof) of service with the clerk that shows exactly how and when the complaint and summons were served on each defendant

If your case was assigned to a District Judge, you may need to include information about the judge's availability. It is best to ask the clerk when they issue your summons. If the complaint is not served within 90 days, the court may dismiss your case. It is helpful to be aware that if you submit a summons by mail, you will need to include a self-addressed stamped envelope so that the signed and sealed summons may be returned (issued) to you. You may also receive instructions on how to prepare a case management statement, which will be covered later. These instructions are generally included in the judges standing orders.

IX. Getting the Defendant to Waive Service

A waiver of service simply means that the defendant agrees to receive papers by mail rather than requiring that they be served in person. Under Rule 4 (m) of the FRCP (Federal Rules of Civil Procedure), you must either obtain a waiver of service, or serve each defendant within 90 days of the filing of the complaint. You will need to have the defendant sign and send back to you a document that is called a “Waiver of Service”. You will then file this waiver with the court. You may not ask for a waiver from an incompetent person or a minor. You also may not request a waiver of service from any government or its employees.

You will need two forms in federal court for a waiver of service:

1. Notice of a lawsuit and a request to waive service of a summons
2. A waiver of the service of summons form

Both of these forms can be downloaded at
https://cand.uscourts.gov/forms/civil-forms/

You will need to send these two completed forms, plus a copy of the complaint, summons, and the above-mentioned forms, plus an extra copy of the waiver request along with a self-addressed stamped envelope via first class mail. If the defendant sends you the signed waiver, you must file these with the court. Keep an extra copy for your records, and the defendant is then considered served.

X. How to Serve the Defendant

Rule 4(c)(2) provides that you cannot serve the defendant yourself, nor can anyone who is a party to the lawsuit.

The defendant may be served:

1. Hand delivered to the defendant
2. Hand delivered to any responsible party who lives at the defendant's home
3. Hand delivered to an agent of the defendant who is authorized to receive service of process (authorized agent)
4. By any other method authorized by state law where the defendant is served.

For example, California Code of Civil Procedure starting at §413.10 authorizes service only by the following:

1. Hand delivered to the defendant
2. Hand delivered to a person over the age of 18 at the home or place of business of the defendant followed by a mailed copy to the defendant at that address
3. By mail followed by an acknowledgement of receipt
4. By newspaper publication with the court's approval

You also have the option of hiring a professional process server to have the defendant served properly. With any option that you choose, you need to be keenly aware that insufficient service of process is grounds for a dismissal of your case, so be aware of the specific process required by your particular jurisdiction. Don't assume and always read carefully before settling on a process. You may also benefit from buying a copy of Black's Law Dictionary for the times when you come across terms that you do not understand. Even if you serve the defendant, you may also be required to serve a registered agent of process if there is one listed such as is common with companies and businesses.

XI. Filing a Certificate of Service

You must file proof of service with the court where you filed your original complaint. Your proof of service should include:

1. The date your papers were served
2. The exact place where service was made
3. Detailed explanation of the method used to complete service
4. Names and addresses of those who were served
5. A list of the documents that were served
6. Dated signature of the person who served the complaint

If a party has an attorney, you are required to serve that person's counsel. The person providing the signature must swear under penalty of perjury that the foregoing statements in the certificate of service are true.

The rules for filing documents other than the complaint are different and can be found in the FRCP Rule 5. You will need a certificate of service for every document that you file and serve. Service can be made by:

1. Handing it to the person (defendant or otherwise)

2. Leaving it at their office with a clerk or home with an adult
3. Mailing it to a last known address
4. By E-mail if the person has consented in writing
5. Any other method for which there is written consent

XII. Responding to a Complaint

You are required to file a written response to a complaint. Answering by the deadline assures that you will not risk a FRCP Rule 55 Default Judgment. You may either file an answer to the complaint or file a motion challenging some aspect of the complaint. You will likely still need to file an answer, but only after the court has ruled on your motion. Responses to a complaint are covered in FRCP Rule 12.

Both parties may agree to extend the deadline to respond to a complaint without the court's approval, but it needs to be in writing. Otherwise, Rule 12(a)(1)(A)(i) provides that the general deadline is 21 days once served. If service has been waived, the FRCP dictates that the time to extend a response must be specified in the waiver of service, otherwise it is 60 days for persons served within the United States and 90 days for those served outside the United States.

An answer should challenge the merits and factual accuracy of the plaintiff's legal entitlement to relief based on the facts as they are presented in the complaint. The format should match the format of the complaint, ie. you should number responses that correspond to each numbered paragraph in the complaint. Specifics for an answer are provided in FRCP

Rule 8(b)(1). You may also download a sample answer packet from here: https://cand.uscourts.gov/pro-se-litigants/legal-help-center-templates-packets/

What is required for most courts is that each sentence, each paragraph, should admit what you admit and deny what you deny. If there is not enough information available to you to admit to a fact, then you should state that in your response. If a fact is partly true, you should admit that fact and deny the rest. If you fail to deny any statement, it will be treated as admitted, so be sure to cover every statement.

You should also include all defenses such as fraud, illegality of a contract, etc. Please refer to your answer packet for details. Under legal rules affirmative defenses may defeat all or portions of the plaintiff's claim. It is up to you to raise any potential defenses. At trial, the defendant will have the burden of proof for defenses. Each affirmative defense should be listed in a separate paragraph at the end of the answer. Any defense not raised in your answer is waived and cannot be later brought up in court, so think about your answer and proceed with caution.

Your answer should also include your prayer for relief. If you think the plaintiff is entitled to something or nothing, your answer should state this. The only way to make your own claim at this point would be with a counterclaim. Counterclaims may be filed with your answer, and certain types of counterclaims may be waived if you don't bring them up now.

You may amend an answer within 21 days of it being served under FRCP Rule 15(a)(1)(or other specified deadline in your local rules) without permission from the court. If the deadline has passed, you may obtain written permission from the other party or file a motion to amend an answer to a complaint.

To file a motion to amend an answer, you should:

1. Draft a new answer and attach it to the motion
2. Your motion to amend should state exactly what has been changed in your answer and state that you are asking permission to change it

If you are entering an entirely new answer, your document should be titled “FIRST AMENDED ANSWER”, and, If you are filing a counterclaim at the same time, your document should be titled “FIRST AMENDED ANSWER AND COUNTERCLAIM”.

XIII. Counterclaims

Compulsory counterclaims are counterclaims that are based on the same events that are the subject of the lawsuit. It may be the same events, contract, or transactions. These types of counterclaims need to be filed with your answer; if they are not you may be waiving your right to bring the claim later. Permissive counterclaims are not based on the same events and need to be filed independently. You must have a separate basis for subject matter jurisdiction and there are no rules that govern time for filing.

The plaintiff's response to a counterclaim is called a "response". FRCP Rule 12(a)(1)(B) requires that the response be filed within 21 days of being served, or you may file a motion pertaining to the counterclaim. Since this counterclaim is really a complaint, you will find similar requirements and will need to challenge the factual accuracy and the merits of the complaint.

XIV. Motions to Challenge the Complaint

If you want to file a Rule 12 motion instead of an answer to the complaint, you will need to do so within the deadline. If you file such a motion you will not need to file your answer until the court rules on your motion.

A Motion to Dismiss argues that there are issues with the way the complaint is written, was filed, or served.

Common challenges to argue in a Motion to Dismiss include:

1. Lack of subject matter jurisdiction - the court has no legal authority to hear the case
2. Lack of personal jurisdiction - there is little connection to the district
3. Improper venue
4. Insufficient process in the preparation of the summons
5. Failure to state a claim for which relief can be granted
6. Failure to join an indispensable party- failure to join a party that must be included

If your motion is denied, you must file an answer within 14 days. If the court rules on your motion with leave to amend, that means that some error exists that the plaintiff may be able to fix. The plaintiff usually has 30 days to file an amended complaint; the amended complaint may be served by mail. If the judge grants the motion with prejudice, that means that there are errors that cannot be fixed. If some, but not all claims in the complaint have been dismissed, the defendant will need to file an answer to the remaining claims within the deadline.

Another Rule 12 motion, motions to strike are used to attack portions of the complaint that are considered immaterial, redundant, scandalous, or impertinent. A motion to strike is covered in FRCP Rule 12(f)(2). You will still need to file an answer to the portions of the complaint not stricken.

XV. Not Responding to a Complaint

Not responding to a complaint means that the plaintiff can seek a default judgment. Under Rule 55 of the FRCP. The plaintiff begins by filing a request for entry of a default judgment along with proof of service to the defendant. This is done in the form of a declaration. Once the clerk approves this, the defendant can no longer file an answer without first filing a motion to set aside default judgment (FRCP Rule 55(c)). Once default judgment is entered, the defendant is assumed to have admitted every fact stated in the complaint except for the amount of damages.

The plaintiff should then file a motion for default judgement supported by:

1. The declaration showing that the defendant was served the complaint but did not file a written response

2. A declaration proving the amount of damages as stated in the complaint (the plaintiff may not include any damages not included in the complaint)

FRCP Rule 58(b) dictates certain rules for minors and incompetent persons in default judgment

The defendant should file a response to the motion for default judgment and also appear at the hearing. The defendant may challenge the sufficiency of service and that the facts stated do not amount to a law violation. He may also challenge the amount of damages contained within the motion for default judgment.

XVI. Relief from Default or Default Judgment

The defendant may make a motion to set aside default judgment under FRCP Rule 55(c). Common reasons to argue include mistake, fraud, or newly discovered evidence. A motion to set aside default judgment should include a detailed explanation of the failure to respond.

XVII. Common Motions

A motion in simple terms is any formal request for something you want the court to do in your case. Motions can also be made by non-parties.

Common motions include:

1. Motions to amend
2. Motions to dismiss
3. Motions for extensions of time
4. Motions for summary judgment
5. Motions to appear by telephone
6. Motions for a more definite statement
7. Motions for a protective order

The moving party files the motion explaining what you want the court to do in detail and chooses a hearing day from the civil law and motion calendar. This date must be at least 35 days from the filing date. The opposing party will file a brief explaining exactly why it believes the motion should not be granted. The opposition brief is due no later than 14 days after the filing date. The moving party may then file a "reply brief" that addresses only the arguments brought up in the opposition brief. The reply brief is due no later than 7 days after the due date of the opposition brief. After the filing of these two briefs, no more documents can be filed pertaining to the motion without permission from the court. The judge may decide on a motion based on the papers alone or the court may hold a hearing where each party will be given a chance to talk about the arguments in their papers. You may not put forward any argument not found in your submitted documents on the matter. The judge will then issue a written decision.

Rule 7 (b) of the FRCP, and various local civil rules dictate what a motion should and should not contain. The court may refuse to consider your motion if you do not follow these specific rules. Motions must be made in writing. Motions should also be no more than 25 pages. You should include the name and contact information of the moving party. They also require a Rule 11 signature. The above mentioned rule also forbids motions from containing facts that are known to be false. You may download a motion packet from the federal court's Legal Help Center at: https://cand.uscourts.gov/pro-se-litigants/legal-help-center-templates-packets/

XVIII. How to Write a Motion

The title of your motion should be "PLAINTIFF"S MOTION FOR....". Under the case number type the date and time as you have already found an available date and time from the motion calendar. Be sure that you chose a date at least 35 days in advance of your motion filing date. Your first paragraph should include a notice of motion, which tells the other parties what you filed and when you have asked the court to hold a hearing. You second paragraph should include your statement of purpose, ie. what you are asking the court to do.

You must include a memorandum of points and authorities that includes a list of issues to be decided and a statement of facts along with legal arguments explaining why the court should grant your motion. If this is longer than 10 pages, you should include a table of contents and a table of authorities that you have cited in your text. Your table of authorities should denote the particular page number where you have cited each authority. The Bluebook Guide to citations is the main authority for in text citations. Make sure your citations adhere to civil rule requirements. Your motion should also include declarations (signed statements sworn under penalty of perjury by persons with personal knowledge). The title of your declaration(s) should read: "DECLARATION OF JS [Full Name] IN SUPPORT OF PLAINTIFF"S MOTION TO DISMISS". Your motion should contain numbered paragraphs. You must sign and date the entire motion and be sure to include page numbers.

You should also include the proposed order for the court that spells out what will happen if the court grants your motion. The order should be titled "PROPOSED ORDER" with a line space for the court's signature. The court could use your order or they may write their own.
You may write a statement of non-opposition to motion, which is due at the same time as the opposition brief. You may request an extension of time to respond to the motion before the deadline has lapsed without a motion, however, if the deadline has lapsed, you will need to write a motion to get an extension. You may also file a motion to shorten time if you need your motion to be heard quickly.

Reply briefs are not to exceed 15 pages and should be titled "REPLY BRIEF IN SUPPORT OF [Name][Date] and [time].

XIX. Motions with Urgent Issues

All parties may stipulate (mutually agree) to shorten time in a written document signed by all parties and filed with a declaration to the court. The declaration should explain why you are requesting that your motion be heard early. It should also list any previous schedule changes in the lawsuit. It should describe the effect the proposed change would have on the case. A proposed order may be submitted, it should be titled "PURSUANT TO STIPULATION, IT IS SO ORDERED....".

XX. Motions to Shorten Time

A motion to shorten time must be under 5 pages and include:

1. Details about why the motion should be heard early
2. Describe the potential harm to you if it is not
3. State efforts made by you to get a stipulation
4. Describe your efforts to comply with FRCP Rule 37 requiring parties to negotiate before filing motions
5. Describe the nature of the dispute in the motion and state positions
6. List all previous schedule adjustments in the case
7. Describe the effects the schedule change would have on your case

Motions to shorten time must be filed no later than 4 days after the motion is received.You will need a copy of the motion, a declaration, and a proposed order.

XXI. A Motion Hearing

In a motion hearing, the moving party has a chance to argue why their motion should be granted. The non-moving party will then have an opportunity to give their arguments as to why the motion should not be granted, if that is their position. You may not argue new points that are not contained within your papers. You should refer to your notes during your argument, but speak directly to the judge. If the judge interrupts with questions, you should answer the question fully, and then return to your argument. Always keep a pen and paper handy during a hearing. Discuss issues with opposing counsel in the hallway and never disrupt the courtroom.

XXII. Initial Disclosures

Initial Disclosures are made by requests to serve initial disclosures, which is based on the best information that you have at that time. However, if you fail to disclose a relevant piece of information, the judge may bar you from using that info at a later time. Be sure that you are aware of the deadline that you have to deliver all the initial disclosures. You will find an Initial Disclosures Packet available for download at the U.S. court's Legal Help Center here:
https://cand.uscourts.gov/pro-se-litigants/legal-help-center-templates-packets/

The initial disclosures must be served within 14 days after your meet and confer (which is covered in FRCP Rule 26 (f). This is usually 21+ days prior to the case management conference referred to in the Complaint section of this text. The parties may stipulate to different times for the due date of initial disclosures if desired by both parties. The court may also order a different due date, if necessary. Initial disclosures are written, signed, and served on all parties.

Your initial disclosures must include:

1. The name and address of every person likely to have information that you may use to support your claims unless you will use them only for impeachment
2. The type of information that each person has
3. Copies or descriptions of each by category
4. All documents that support your calculations of damages
5. Copies of insurance agreements that may cover any award for damages

You must notify the other parties promptly if you discover evidence that needs to be disclosed. If you do need to supplement, your document should be titled “SUPPLEMENTAL” or “AMENDED INITIAL DISCLOSURES”. If you fail to disclose in a timely manner, you may not be able to use that information later at trial.

XXIII. Case Management Conference

This is held to set a schedule for the case including a trial date. It is usually given to the plaintiff when the complaint is filed. The parties must meet and confer at least 21 days before the case management conference (CMC). At your CMC, be prepared to discuss the basis for your claim and whether early settlement is an option for you. You will normally discuss a timeline for initial disclosures under FRCP Rule 46(a)(1) during this conference. You should exchange with the other party the names of any and all persons that are likely to have information pertaining to the case. Parties should be able to reach an agreement on how and when discovery will be complete. You may agree to an alternative dispute process, such as mediation or a settlement conference. Parties should prepare a joint (or separate) case management statement that informs the court of the results of the parties discussion. The statement should comply with any standing judges orders concerning the CMC statement.

A proposed discovery plan is a written proposal about how and when discovery should be conducted. The judge will review this plan and will determine how to proceed in a case management order that will be written. The parties must show a good faith effort to negotiate and agree on a discovery plan, and iron out any timing issues, objections, and particular issues. You must attend a CMC in person unless you get permission in writing to attend by telephone. Requests for this must be received no more than 5 days before the conference.

XXIV. Methods of Discovery

Discovery is a way to ask for information, and to receive it. There are six main types of discovery that you should become familiar with. They are depositions, interrogatories, requests for production, mental examinations, physical examinations, and requests for admission. Discovery may begin immediately following the date that the judge sends out the case management order, but it is almost always after the meet and confer. If for some reason, you find the need to start discovery earlier than this you should try to come to a mutual agreement to begin earlier. The limits to discovery include privileged information, such as communications between a lawyer and a client, and doctor-patient communications.

Disclosure may also be limited if:

1. The information is readily available and is easy for either party to attain
2. A party has had multiple chances to receive the same information but hasn't
3. The proposed benefit is not greater than the burden
4. The information is otherwise privileged

FRCP Rule 26(b) imposes scope and limits on the number or requests, so be sure to stay keenly aware and choose each request carefully.

XXV. Depositions

Depositions are question-answer sessions that are conducted outside of the courtroom. The answers are recorded by audio, audio-visual, or stenographic means by a court reporter. Rule 30 of the FRCP covers depositions in detail. The person is under oath and is referred to as the deponent. A deponent can be any person and does not need to be a party to the lawsuit. The questions can be written or administered by telephone. The party who is taking the deposition is responsible for the cost. It is also up to that party to obtain the transcript.

You do not need the court's permission to take a deposition unless:

1. The deponent is in prison
2. Your side has already taken more than 10 without any stipulation from the other side
3. The same deponent has already been deposed without any stipulation
4. Your deposition would take place before the meet and confer

The rules are different if the deponent would be out of town following the meet and confer. In that case, you may not need the court's permission to hold a deposition prior to the meet and confer. You must serve the deponent a written notice of the deposition, which also must be served on all parties.

The notice of deposition must include:

1. The name and address of the deponent - or if not known an adequate description ie. "the night shift clerk at the A&M".
2. If the deponent is a business, then the business must give you the name and address of the person who will give testimony
3. The method of recording
4. Your address and signature pursuant to FRCP Rule 26(g)(1)

Non-party deponents must be served with a subpoena to appear at a deposition. Blank forms for a subpoena to testify at a deposition can be downloaded here: https://cand.uscourts.gov/forms/civil-forms/

The subpoena may be served by any person over the age of 18 who is not a party to the suit. The subpoena must be hand delivered along with the fees for one day attendance.The party who is responsible for the cost of the deposition must also pay travel expenses for the deponent according to 28 U.S.C. § 1821 and 41.

A party or non-party may file a motion to quash a subpoena if there is an undue burden or expense to the deponent. The court must quash the subpoena if it would require the deponent to travel more than 100 miles to testify at the deposition. The court will then issue an order that the person does not have to appear. If you are a party to the lawsuit, you are required to appear at a deposition if you are served. If the time and date would cause a particular inconvenience for you, you should notify the other parties immediately. The transcripts of a deposition can be admitted as evidence in a civil trial.

If you are the deponent and have to testify at a deposition, you should review all your documents carefully prior to the deposition. Ask for clarity on any questions that cause confusion to you. Try to focus on answering the questions completely even if another thought comes to mind. You will be allowed to add additional information at the end that you feel is important but was not covered.

A subpoena duces tecum requires someone to produce copies of documents or other things at the deposition. The documents that you want present should be listed in the notice of deposition and the subpoena duces tecum. FRCP Rule 32(b) covers these topics. Under Rule 30(d)(1), the deposition can last no longer than 7 hours over the course of 1 day. You are allowed to state any legal objections in a deposition such as, the question was too vague, the question was several questions rolled into one, or that the question was argumentative. You may also state if the information is something that you are not able to give for legal reasons. You may object, however, you will still need to answer the question. You do not have to answer if the question would violate a privilege. Depositions can be interrupted for a party to make a motion on the grounds that the deposition is not being conducted in good faith, or that it is intended to harass, embarrass, or oppress the deponent. FRCP Rule 30(d)(3) covers these scenarios.

The deponent has 30 days from the time that the transcript is complete to review and make any changes to their responses. They must state the changes that are being made and the reasons.

XXVI. Interrogatories

Interrogatories are written questions that must be answered in writing and under oath. Sample interrogatories can be found here: https://cand.uscourts.gov/pro-se-litigants/legal-help-center-templates-packets/

Any party may serve up to 25 interrogatories without the court's permission. If you need to go over this limit you may file a motion asking the court to permit more. Interrogatories only cover non-privileged material. The questions must be written out and numbered and you have to answer them within 30 days. You must also include a Rule 26(g)(1) signature. A relevant federal civil rule requires that each question must be written out before a response is stated. You may answer or object, or both, within the same question. You may not say that you do not know if the answer is available to you. If the answer exists somewhere in your records, then you are required to find the answer. If the answer is extremely easy to locate, then you may state where it can be found. You may request more time to file your answers or file a motion requesting an extension. Objections should be stated in writing and signed. Interrogatories must be signed by the party whether you have a lawyer or not. If you later learn that your answer is incomplete, you must file a supplement to your original answers. FRCP Rule 26(e)(1) covers this topic.

XXVII. Requests for Document Production

Requests for document production include all documents whether hard copies or those that are electronically stored. This includes e-mails or messages which may prove or defend your case. The documents are those which you reasonably believe the defendant has and that contain information that is pertinent to your claim. Requests for document production can be served on anyone, not just a party to the lawsuit. A sample Request for Documents is available here: https://cand.uscourts.gov/pro-se-litigants/legal-help-center-templates-packets/

If the person is a party to the lawsuit, FRCP Rules 34(a) and (b) apply. The request will allow you to inspect any document in their possession, custody, or control. It also includes requests for tangible things, that you may copy, test, or sample anything in their possession, custody, or control. Finally, you may file a request to be allowed access to the inspection of a property meaning that you may survey, measure, or sample anything at the specified property.

Your request must list the items that you want to inspect and provide enough detail that the person would easily know what it is that you are asking to inspect. Each request must be numbered separately and signed. There is no limit to the number of requests as long as it does not present an undue burden. The request may be served by any method listed in Rule 5(b).

XXVIII. Responding to a Request for Document Production

You must respond within 30 days of being served a request for document production unless the court has authorized some other deadline. You also must rewrite every response in full before your response or objection. You may state that you will allow inspection of the item at a specified date and time. If you object to any of the individual requests, you will need to state the reasons and whether you have withheld the items on the same basis, and state that you will allow inspection of the rest. The items must be presented in the order as they are requested, and labeled, or presented as they are found in the normal course of business. The items must be produced by the time specified within the request or another reasonable time specified in the response. Rules 34(c)and 45 cover requests to non-parties. FRCP 45 handles the issuing, service, and responding to a subpoena duces tecum (SDT).

Under Rule 45(b)(1), you must take steps to avoid undue burden or expense on the person being served a STD. For federal lawsuits, the same form is used for a SDT as it is with a deposition subpoena. The person served has 14 days to file written objections to the subpoena. If an objection is made, the parties should meet to resolve the issue if possible. If no resolution is made, the serving party may need a court order to inspect the documents. (FRCP Rule 45(d)(2)(B). The person being served a SDT only has to actually appear at a deposition.

XXIX. Requests for Admissions

A request for admissions is to ask a party to admit the truthfulness of a fact that has a connection to the lawsuit. This may be a fact or a set of facts, an application of the law to a fact or facts, or their opinions about these. It may also ask for an admittance about the genuineness of a document. Requests for admissions may only be served on parties to the lawsuit. The court will take anything in admissions as proven. Requests for admissions should be in numbered paragraphs to make responses easier to decipher and respond to. Requests for admissions should be signed and certified.

There is no limitation in a federal civil context to the number of requests for admissions you can serve, within reason. As with other court documents, you should state each request in full before your response. You should also state your reasons for objections. Normally, you will have 30 days to respond unless the deadline is otherwise dictated by court order. If no response is filed within 30 days, all requests for admissions are treated as admitted.

In a response for a request for admission, you should explain in detail why you cannot admit or deny a request. If you can only admit in part, admit what you can and explain your denial for the rest. While the facts can be treated as admitted, it is only for the purposes of that lawsuit; the facts cannot be used for the purposes of a separate lawsuit. If a party fails to deny a fact that is later proven true, the other side may be able to recover expenses associated with the cost of proving that fact.

The court must grant the prevailing party those expenses unless:

1. The request was objectionable
2. The admissions were unimportant
3. The party who did not admit to the facts had a reason to believe he might prevail on that point
4. There are other valid reasons for the failure to admit

XXX. Mental or Physical Examinations

A party might request a party to submit to a mental or physical examination when a particular condition is at issue in the lawsuit. The requesting party must pay the expenses for the exam. The communications between the examiner and the person submitting to the exam are not privileged or confidential. The requesting party may only request a mental or physical exam by filing a motion.

The motion should:

1. Explain why there is a need
2. Explain the time, place, scope and conditions of the proposed exam
3. Identify the person who will be conducting the exam

The person may request a written detailed report about the examiner's findings themselves, and the report will be admitted to the document records. If appropriate, there may be an additional need to request further medical records following the results of the exam.

XXXI. Motion for a Protective Order

A motion for a protective order is a motion asking the judge to order discovery be carried out a particular way. It may seek to impose some type of limitation on discovery. Motions for a protective order may be filed in the court where a deposition is supposed to take place, rather than the court where the lawsuit is pending.

Motions for a protective order must include:

1. A certification that the party has tried to confer to resolve the issue before filing a motion
2. An explanation of the dispute and what you want the court to do
3. An explanation of facts and law that would make it appropriate for the court to grant your motion

If an issue arises during a discovery event (a conference to discuss details of discovery) and it raises an urgent issue, some districts allow you to call the chambers to arrange a telephone conference. If you still have not made sufficient progress there are a few motions that can be filed to address a no-response situation. These can be referred to as procedural motions.

XXXII. Motion to Compel

A motion to compel can result positively in the judge ordering the party to respond or to make disclosures. This is covered under Rule 37 of the FRCP. A motion to compel to a non-party should be filed in the district court where the discovery is taking place.

The motion to compel should include:

1. A certification that you tried in good faith to get the person to respond or disclose
2. A detailed explanation of the problem and what you want the court to do
3. The complete text of every disputed request followed by the complete text of a disputed response (if applicable)
4. An explanation of the facts and law that point to why you think the court should grant your motion

The party against whom the motion was filed pays the expenses unless:

1. The motion was filed without first making an attempt
2. The non-response was substantially justified
3. There is something that make the award of expense unjust

XXXIII. Motion for Sanctions

A motion for sanctions asks the court to punish the person for not making the required disclosures. This motion must be made where the lawsuit is pending.

Discovery sanctions can be initiated for the failure to:

1. Provide the required disclosures
2. Obey a court order
3. Appear for a deposition
4. Answer interrogatories
5. Respond to a request for production

Procedural motions must be:

1. Filed as a separate motion
2. Set for the normal 35 day (as per Civil Rule in your jurisdiction) schedule for a hearing
3. Made as soon as possible after learning of the deficiency
4. Not field more than 14 days after an entry of judgment

These motions must contain:

1. Certification that you have tried in good faith
2. Explanation of the problem and why the court should grant your motion
3. The facts and Law
4. Explanation of the circumstances that support your motion

5. Detailed description of the efforts you made to gain compliance
6. Itemized and detailed descriptions for attorneys fees including hourly rate

Granted motions for sanctions may result in:

1. An order resolving issues of fact favorable to the moving party
2. The prohibition of evidence related to claims or defenses relative to the questioned facts
3. The striking of certain documents from the case or staying the case until the order is obeyed
4. The dismissal of the lawsuit or a default judgment
5. Civil contempt of court

XXXIV. Motions for Summary Judgment

A motion for summary judgment asks the court to resolve the case without trial when there is no dispute about the relevant facts. Where there is a genuine dispute about key facts, summary judgment is not appropriate. When a plaintiff files a motion for summary judgment, the point is to show that the undisputed facts undeniably show that the defendant broke the law. When the defendant files, he intends to show that the plaintiff does not have the undisputed evidence necessary to prove every element of her claim.

Motions for Summary Judgment Key points:

1. Can include individual claims or the entire lawsuit
2. If the motion is granted, the lawsuit is over

3. The motion should only be granted if no reasonable jury could find in favor of the opposing party
4. The judge will consider all admissible evidence
5. The judge considers the motion in a light most favorable to the opposing party
6. A denial means that there are disputed facts
7. Unless the parties agree to settle the matter, a denial means it will go to trial
8. Some judges only allow one such motion per side

In an opposition to a motion or summary judgment, you should dispute the plaintiff's version of the facts and present your own. You will serve the opposition brief the same as you would any other motion. To succeed on a motion for summary judgement, the plaintiff should try to show that the defendant does not have evidence that, if true, would prove a valid defense to the plaintiff's claim. To counter this, the defendant must submit admissible evidence that shows there is a factual dispute about at least one element that is required to prove the plaintiff's claim. Affirmative defenses are a complete defense. The defendant should raise those when he or she is the moving party.

The judge will only consider admissible evidence. Every fact that you rely on should be supported by evidence. You should file copies of the evidence that you want the court to consider. When citing a document, you should point the judge to the page number and corresponding line. The court does not have to look at any documents that are not included in your brief. The court does not search other evidence provided at different times.You must present all the evidence you want considered on your summary judgment motion.

An affidavit or a declaration of a statement of fact signed under oath can be used as evidence supporting or opposing a motion for summary judgment. An affidavit must be sworn before a notary public. Applications and declarations are covered under FRCP Rule 56(c), and must be made by someone with personal first-hand knowledge. They may show their competence to the court by testifying to the facts. They should only state facts which are admissible. You may obtain blank declaration forms here: https://cand.uscourts.gov/pro-se-litigants/legal-help-center-templates-packets/

Unrepresented parties should be aware that hearsay (second hand evidence) is not admissible in federal court per the Federal Rules of Evidence 801-807. Documents such as letters, records, and e-mails are called exhibits, and you must prove that they are genuine. These types of documents need to be authenticated by sworn statements as to their genuineness and authenticity before they are considered admissible. Keep this in mind if you plan to rely on them when preparing a motion for summary judgment, or an opposition brief.

A statement of undisputed facts is a list of facts that all parties agree are true and that contains citations to these facts that lets the judge know these facts are true. The statement of undisputed facts must be signed by all parties and will be taken by the judge as true. Some civil rules do not allow separate statements of undisputed facts, so you need to locate the relevant rules for your jurisdiction.

Motions for summary judgment can be filed at any time as long as there is no particular deadline set by the judge. Usually the plaintiff must wait 20 days after the complaint is filed to make a motion for summary judgment. Most of these motions occur later in a case because they rely heavily on evidence obtained during discovery. Refer to FRCP Rule 56(d) if you need more time for discovery. You will need to convey why you do not already have the evidence and state exactly what additional discoveries you need and how it relates.

XXXV. Disclosures Before Trial - Expert Witness Reports

Rules surrounding disclosures before trial are intended to allow the defendant to prepare for trial and to avoid surprises for all parties. A written report must be made and served at least 90 days before trial. Refer to FRCP Rule 26(a)(2) and (a)(3) for specifics on the written report. Your report must include a written report that is prepared and signed by the witness. Expert disclosures must be made before the deadline, but at least 90 days before trial begins. If your witness will be presented solely to contradict information in an expert witness report, it is due no later than 30 days following the disclosure.

The expert witness report must contain:

1. A complete statement of all opinions he or she intends to use at trial along with the basis and reasons

2. Data or other evidence the expert used to form these opinions
3. All exhibits they intend to use to support these opinions
4. List of qualifications including all publications in the previous 10 years
5. The amount of personal compensation offered in exchange for testimony.
6. A list of all other cases in the previous 4 years of which he or she has testified or been a deponent

The report must be signed and served on all parties, but does not need to be filed with the federal district court. Check jurisdictional specific rules to be certain you are following proper procedure. If, after the expert witness report has been filed, you find that it contains incorrect or incomplete information, refer to Rule 26 (e)(1) and (e)(2) on how to supplement your report. This will be due no later than all other pretrial disclosures.

XXXVI. Witness and Exhibit Lists

Per FRCP Rule 26(a)(3), you will need to file and serve a witness and exhibit list at least 30 days before trial.

Your exhibit and witness list should include:

1. Names, addresses, and telephone numbers of each witness (identified separately) that you either intend to present or may present at trial
2. The identities of all witnesses by deposition - you may include the relevant portions of the transcript

3. The identification of each document or exhibit you will use or plan to use if the need arises

Witnesses and documents that will only be used to impeach need not be disclosed in your list. All pretrial disclosures must be in writing.

XXXVII. Jury Trial

If the type of case you have allows for a jury trial, and at least one of the parties has requested one, then that is how your case will be decided if you do not prevail with your motion for summary judgment. If you fail to request a jury trial, you will forfeit that right. If your case does not qualify for a jury trial as a right, your case will be decided at a bench trial without a jury. Trials are typically held within 18 months of the filing of your complaint. During trial, both parties will give their opening statements, then each will be able to argue their case. The rebuttal is where you will have the chance to refute evidence put on by the other side. Then, each party gives their closing arguments.

Initially, the judge will be given the first opportunity to release any jurors believed to have personal or financial hardships that would make it difficult to perform a juror's job. Next, parties will have the chance to convince the judge that a particular juror would be too biased to be fair and ask that these jurors also be excused. This is called a challenge for cause. Lastly, each party will be given a limited number of pre-emptory challenges where they may dismiss a limited number of jurors for any reason.

Your opening statements should describe the particular issues and state what they intend to prove. The jury should be able to understand what it is that each party considers important. You must not mention any issues that have been excluded from trial.

Each party will be allowed to directly examine and cross-examine each witness until they have no more questions. During a re-direct, you will only be allowed to ask about topics that were covered in a cross-examination.

If a party fails to object, for example, to improper evidence, the judge may allow that evidence to be presented. The opposing party will not be able to raise that question on appeal, so it is crucial that you pay close attention and be prepared. It is the party's responsibility to bring to the judge's attention any errors and allow him or her to correct them.

You should stand and briefly state your objection. Do not explain or give arguments. You may be called to a sidebar to discuss the issue outside of the jury's presence. Your objection will be sustained or overruled.

XXXVIII. Motion for Judgment as a Matter of Law

After the plaintiff has put on all of their evidence, they may file a motion for judgment as a matter of law. These motions are covered in the FRCP Rule 50(a). In filing a motion for judgement as a matter of law, the plaintiff believes that he or she has put on enough evidence and facts to be entitled to judgment no matter what the defendant is able to show. Or, when a defendant files this motion, even with the plaintiff's evidence, if taken as true, he or she would not be able to persuade a reasonable jury to decide in their favor.

The judge may put off ruling on this motion until after the defendant has put on his entire case. Otherwise, each will give their closing arguments. If these motions are denied, the parties will wait for a jury verdict (must be unanimous in federal court), or the findings of fact and law that will be written by the judge.

XXXIX. Motion for Reconsideration

Motions for reconsideration must be filed before the court enters a final judgment and may be made only with the court's decision in my particular court of study. Check your local rules and standing orders for particulars for your case. When filing a motion for reconsideration, you are essentially saying that the facts or law previously presented were wrong in some kind of an important way, and that this could not have been revealed at the time of the court's order.

Motions for reconsideration may be appropriate when either/or:

1. Important new facts have emerged or there has been a significant change in the law since the order was entered
2. The court clearly failed to consider material and relevant facts, evidence, or key legal points that were presented to the court before the order was issued.

In your motion, you may not merely repeat arguments, and if you do, you will risk court ordered sanctions. No response is necessary and you should use the normal 35 day motion schedule. The parties may file an opposition or reply brief. If granted, the court may vacate the original order, or issue an entirely new order or amended version.

XL. Renewed Motion for Judgment as a Matter of Law

This is a post-judgment motion that can be made only if you filed a motion or judgment as a matter of law at the close of all the evidence, and that motion was denied. This motion essentially says that you believe there was a serious mistake made by the jury and that you made a motion or judgment but was denied under Rule 50(b). In this motion, you must argue that the jury erred in their decision because no reasonable jury could have reached that decision.

The court may rule to:

1. Refuse to disturb the verdict
2. Grant a new trial
3. Direct entry as a matter of law

XLI. Motion for a New Trial

Either party may file a motion requesting a new trial because they believe the first one was flawed. The court is allowed to grant a new trial if the jury's verdict was against the weight of the evidence. The judge will assess the credibility of witnesses and is not required to review the evidence in a light more favorable to any party. The judge will not overturn the verdict unless he is absolutely convinced that a serious mistake was made. In a bench trial, the judge must have made a clear factual error or new evidence has emerged that would have affected the outcome. If the motion is granted, there is not always a need to hold a whole new trial. It can amend the findings of fact, make new findings, or enter a new judgment.

XLII. Motion to Amend or Alter a Judgment

A motion to amend or alter a judgment is also a post-judgment motion. It seeks to change something in the final judgment because of errors during the trial. There must be a clear error that was committed or an intervening change in the relevant law.

XLIII. Motion for Relief from Judgment or Order

A motion for relief from judgment does not argue that the court or jury erred in their decision, but asks the court not to require them to obey the order. FRCP Rule 60(a) allows the court to correct any clerical errors at any time. This is usually limited to minor errors.

A motion for relief from judgment or order can be granted when:

1. Discovered evidence that could not have been discovered in time for a new trial
2. Mistake, misconduct, surprise, or excusable neglect
3. Fraud or misrepresentation by the other party

4. The judgement has been satisfied, released, or a prior judgment on which it was based has been reversed
5. Any other reason justifying relief - only under extraordinary circumstances

Motions for relief from judgment or order must be made within 1 year of the final judgment or other reasonable time specified by the court. This process may be different if it involves review of a magistrate judge's decision.

XLIV. Review of a Magistrate Judge's Decision

There are different rules for review of a magistrate judge's decision. If you did not consent to the case being handled by a magistrate judge, there will be a referring district judge. Objections to a magistrate judge's orders must be filed with the judge who made the referral within 14 days of the decision. You need not file a response. The judge may set aside any part of the order they find to be contrary to the law. You may file a written objection or motion within 14 days. Limit your objections to the parts of the order where you find there to be error. Any party may file a motion asking the district judge to hear additional evidence that was not heard by the magistrate judge. The referring judge makes a de novo review of that portion, which means they will look at the issues from scratch. Use the motion to have the judge look at additional evidence, if desired, or you may use all of the evidence presented to the magistrate. The referring judge may accept, reject, modify, recommend, or send the case back for further review.

All final judgments in federal court can be appealed to the U.S. Court of Appeals in the appropriate circuit. You may refer to the Federal Rules of Appellate Procedure once you decide to appeal your case. Appeals must be filed within 30 days of an entry of judgment.

Guide to Pro Se Civil Litigation - ISBN 979-8-3303-1966-4
Guide to Pro Se Civil Litigation: Research and Writing - ISBN 979-8-3495-4568-9
Guide to Pro Se Civil Litigation - Ebook - ISBN 979-8-3302-2907-9
Guide to Pro Se Civil Litigation: Research and Writing Ebook ISBN 979-8-3495-4571-9

www.ingramcontent.com/pod-product-compliance
Lightning Source LLC
LaVergne TN
LVHW060215210926
848481LV00009B/2748
* 9 7 9 8 3 3 0 3 1 9 6 6 4 *